THE CRAZY WORLD OF

FOOTBALL

CARTOONS BY

Bilstott

EXLEY

NEW YORK • WATFORD, UK

Other cartoon giftbooks in this series:
The Crazy World of Cats (Bill Stott)
The Crazy World of Gardening (Bill Stott)
The Crazy World of Golf (Mike Scott)
The Crazy World of Housework (Bill Stott)
The Crazy World of Marriage (Bill Stott)
The Crazy World of Rugby (Bill Stott)
The Crazy World of Sex (Bill Stott)

First published in hardback in the USA in 1996 by Exley Giftbooks.
Published in Great Britain in 1996 by Exley Publications Ltd.

12 11 10 9 8 7 6 5

Copyright © Bill Stott, 1990

ISBN 1-85015-771-5
The moral right of the author has been asserted.

Printed in China.

Exley Publications Ltd, 16 Chalk Hill, Watford, Herts, WD1 4BN, United Kingdom.
Exley Publications LLC, 232 Madison Avenue, Suite 1206, NY 10016, USA.

"Like it? That's one of the first soccer chants I ever wrote."

"How was the match, Honey?"

"Terrible. We won ten nil. No crowd trouble. No sending-offs. No nothing!"

"I hate it when the referee is fair and you still get beaten..."

"Offside, Kevin..."

"First – my mother and father are married. Second – you were definitely offside. Third – any more language like that and I'll smack your legs!"

③

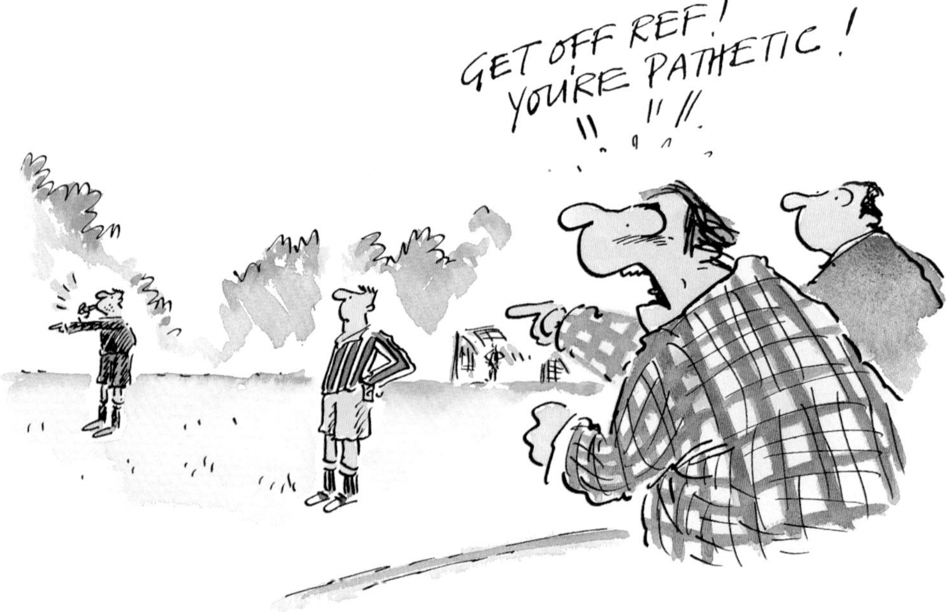
GET OFF REF! YOU'RE PATHETIC!

"Isn't that Saturday's ref?"

"Huh – seven nil. We don't support our team. We prop them up!"

"They're bound to do that – the only other time they line up together is to face a free kick..."

"It's that new signing Boss – the chaps are just making sure he knows
how to roll about and scream in agony at the slightest contact
with an opposing player..."

"Now! Inside! Inside! Lay it back! Go inside! No! Not that way!...

...Sometimes I might as well talk to myself!"

"Great goal, Gary. Gary? ...Where's Gary?"

"There's a guy in the dugout wants a word with you.
He's a Hollywood talent scout..."

"We can't have your number six's mother rushing on every time he's brought down..."

"Gerald likes to practise his card technique before a game."

"I don't suppose there's anything in the rules about that, Ref?"

"Offside? Offside? The guy is blind – he is BLIND!!"

②

"Pardon?"

"Er, I was just saying what a brave decision that was...."

"I told you St. Dominic's were a hard lot – that's their mascot."

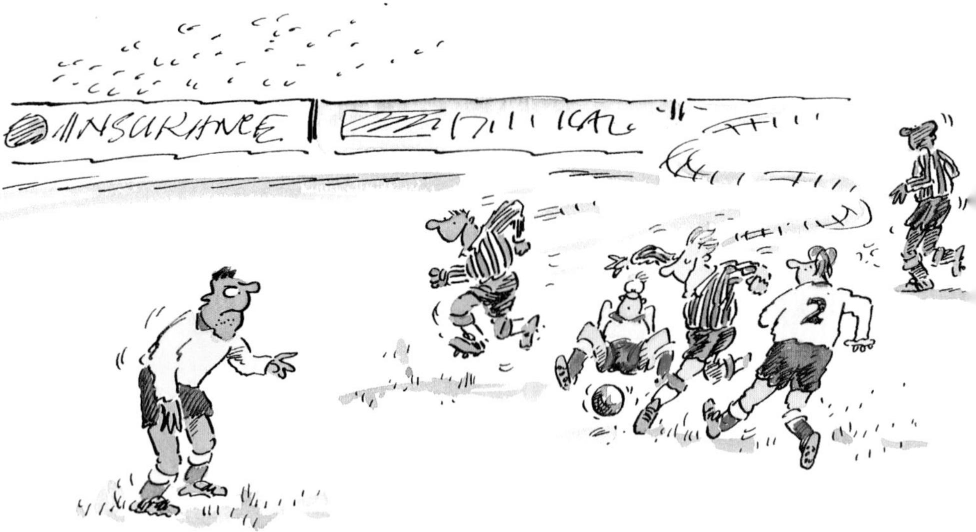
INSURANCE

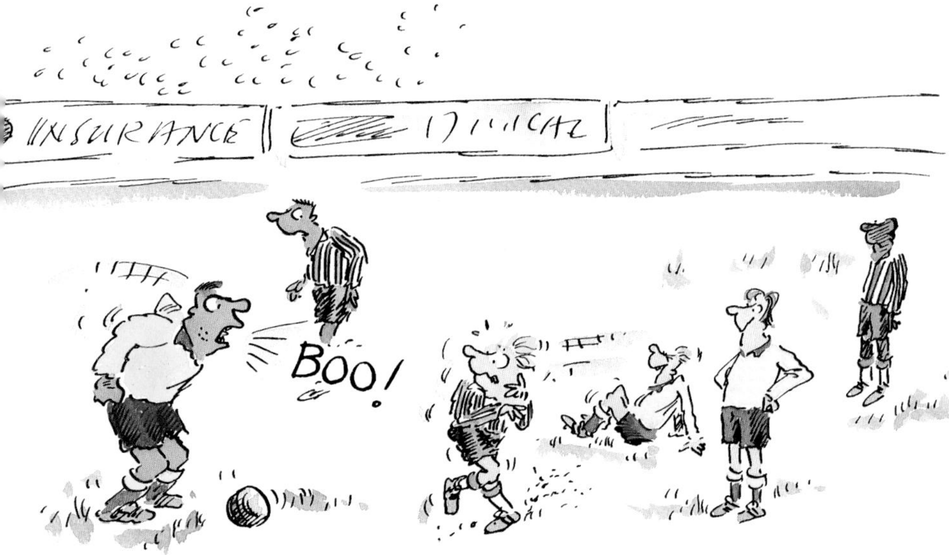
INSURANCE
BOO!

"Smile...!"

"It's Terry's one hundredth sending-off!"

"Their No. 7 was good, wasn't he?"

"Well Brian, at the end of the day, the ref's decision is final, despite him being a two-faced, lying rat who's probably on the take."

"And from here I can see that Rover's No. 7 isn't happy with that decision..."

"Well, we've had a pretty lively debate here tonight..."

"O.K. I want a nice open pattern – Dean and Gary making runs down the flanks, Tommo and Wayne drawing in their defenders. While all this is going on, you Eric, will run about kicking anybody you don't recognize..."

"Look! A sponsor's a sponsor – now put it on!"

"He's going through his after-goal crowd adulation response..."

"Er – what I said about women physios – it was a joke – right?"

"Your million dollar bargain just tied his own bootlaces together."

"Why are we out of the Cup? Well, I think it's because our team's useless and we've scored once in nineteen matches..."

"A <u>free</u> transfer – good grief, no! We're <u>paying</u> you to go!"

"He was showing the kids some advanced tackling techniques..."

"Look. Just because your grandpa bought the ball
doesn't mean he gets to play!"

"Dad says it's got no atmosphere if you watch it indoors..."

"Huh! They've even got better <u>names</u> than us!"

"Guatemala v Equador...Oh goody!"

"I said, 'My mother's coming to stay for a month. The kids have run away to join the Moonies and your car's on fire!'"

"Do you think that if I took up soccer, your dad would do that to me?"

"His dad's very worried about him – he wants a referee's outfit for Christmas!"

"Then Grandad said 'Here's one I bet they don't teach you at school' and kicked it straight through the French window..."

"Our Gary's soccer crazy – he's out in the yard
trying out his dives..."

"See! I told you he could write!"

"Youth Club is organizing a 'Dads' and Lads'' match. I was wondering if you'd care to...

... be a linesman?"

"I'm especially proud of that one – goalie's teeth, semi final, 1963..."

Books in the "Crazy World" series

The Crazy World of Cats (Bill Stott)
The Crazy World of Football (Bill Stott)
The Crazy World of Gardening (Bill Stott)
The Crazy World of Golf (Mike Scott)
The Crazy World of Housework (Bill Stott)
The Crazy World of Marriage (Bill Stott)
The Crazy World of Rugby (Bill Stott)
The Crazy World of Sex (Bill Stott)

Books in the "Fanatic's" series

The Fanatic's Guides are perfect presents for
everyone with a hobby that has got out of hand.
Over fifty hilarious colour cartoons by Roland Fiddy.

The Fanatic's Guide to Cats
The Fanatic's Guide to Computers
The Fanatic's Guide to Dads
The Fanatic's Guide to D.I.Y.
The Fanatic's Guide to Golf
The Fanatic's Guide to Husbands
The Fanatic's Guide to Love
The Fanatic's Guide to Sex

Great Britain: Order these super books from
your local bookseller or from Exley Publications Ltd,
16 Chalk Hill, Watford, Herts WD1 4BN.
(Please send £1.30 to cover postage and packing
on 1 book, £2.60 on 2 or more books.)